Father Still Knows Best

The Wit and Wisdom of America's Favorite TV Dads

Tripp Whetsell

CITADEL PRESS
Kensington Publishing Corp.
www.kensingtonbooks.com

This book is lovingly dedicated to Bill Whetsell for being a wonderful dad who has always wanted what's best for his son and to Uncle Porter for being like a second father and my closest confidant.

It is also dedicated to my beloved friend Sharon Klein for being the person she is and granting me the privilege to be part of her life.

CITADEL PRESS BOOKS are published by

Kensington Publishing Corp.
850 Third Avenue
New York, NY 10022

First printing: May 2005

10 9 8 7 6 5 4 3 2 1

Printed in the United States of America

CIP data is available at the Library of Congress.

ISBN 0-8065-2712-9

Introduction

**The only fathers that don't yell at their kids
are on television.**

—Wally Cleaver, *Leave It to Beaver*

I love my dad and he loves me, although like most fathers and sons we've had our fair share of spirited debates over the years. Nothing major, mind you—and thankfully we've always managed to make up—but suffice it to say we haven't always seen eye to eye.

Women, sports, politics, religion, money, that time in the eighth grade when I tried to spike my hair up like Rod Stewart's. Pick any subject or scenario, and my old man and I probably butted heads. The ironic part is that neither of us was ever completely wrong—just too stubborn and set in our ways to compromise (ask my mother). In the end, the only thing either of us wanted was to assert his independence. Me, to prove I knew everything; my dad, to prevent me from doing something stupid, which I probably would have if he hadn't stopped me.

Did our haggling make our relationship stronger? Maybe, maybe not, but at the risk of getting too psychological, I will say that it's probably what made me an avid TV watcher at a very young age, and ultimately an entertainment journalist by vocation. Whenever the arguments between my father and me got too heated, my first response was always to try to work them out through my favorite television programs. I had no reason to believe that Ward Cleaver (*Leave It to Beaver*), Jim Anderson (*Father Knows Best*), and Andy Taylor (*The Andy Griffith Show*) didn't have all the answers or that Howard Cunningham (*Happy Days*), Cliff Huxtable (*The Cosby Show*), and Jason Seaver (*Growing Pains*) weren't infallible. Even so, I was often disappointed because, unlike Opie, Theo, the Beaver, and their dads, *our* problems could never be resolved in thirty minutes.

Of course, now that I've gotten older—and hopefully, somewhat wiser about the ways of the world—the reality of what was then my boyhood fantasy has finally set in. Nevertheless, I still love these shows I was reared on, and I'll watch them religiously in reruns, repeating the dialog almost verbatim as I do. They never fail to amuse me. And it never ceases to amaze me that a lot of what these TV dads had to say still holds up after all these years. That's a big reason why I wrote this book: to share with like-minded TV junkies these pearls of wisdom—and even some of the jabber—that spewed from the lips of our favorite television fathers.

For me, writing this book has been as much a trip down memory lane as it has been an endless word processing exercise. It is my hope that you will enjoy these quotes from the beloved TV dads you grew up with and want to celebrate again.

After all, for more than half a century they have, by default, tutored us in geometry, taken us on fishing trips, and helped us pick out our first car. They have chaperoned Cub Scout campouts, read us the funny papers, helped us with our science projects, and coached our Little League teams. They have walked us down the aisle, taught us how to defend ourselves against school bullies, given us the facts on the facts of life, and lovingly guided us through the difficult transitions of childhood, adolescence, and adulthood. In short, they have indirectly taught us by compassionate example the fine art of being a human being.

And that's why Father—especially the TV kind—*still* knows best after all these years.

Acceptance

The most important thing for anyone to know is that people can love us just the way we are.

> Fred Rogers, *Mister Rogers' Neighborhood*

The only reason I got in here was because I had enough green to cover my black.

> George Jefferson, *The Jeffersons*

Accidents

When **an accident** does occur, you clear it up immediately.

> **Mike Brady,** *The Brady Bunch*

D.J. CONNER: Was I an accident?
ROSEANNE CONNER: No, D.J., you were a surprise.
D.J.: Oh. What's the difference?
ROSEANNE: Well, an accident is something that you wouldn't do over **again** if you had the chance. A surprise is something you didn't even know you wanted until you got it.
D.J.: Oh. Was Darlene an accident?
DAN CONNER: No, Darlene was a disaster.

> *Roseanne*

Adam and Eve

You don't believe me, read your Bible. Read your story of Adam and Eve. They had it pretty soft in Paradise. They had no problems. They didn't even know they was naked. But Eve, she wasn't satisfied with that, see, and then one day, against direct orders, she made poor Adam eat that apple. God got sore: He told them to keep their clothes on and get the hell out of here.

Archie Bunker, *All in the Family*

Aging

You're never too old to do goofy stuff.

Ward Cleaver, *Leave It to Beaver*

FRED HORTON: Getting old is such a gradual thing that you don't really notice it. You don't look in the mirror and say, "I look older today than yesterday."
LOU GRANT: One day you turn on the football game and the quarterback looks like your grandson.
FRED: Or younger.

Lou Grant

Marge, old people don't need companionship. They need to be

isolated and studied so it can be determined what nutrients they have that might be extracted for our personal use.

> Homer Simpson, *The Simpsons*

Popular belief has it that anybody who's lived fifty or more years is over the hill in every way. The older person is pictured as cranky, exhausted emotionally, economically, sexually, and financially . . . deprived of vitality in general. Ironically, the population of older people is growing with leaps and bounds. Whether we like it or not, old age is what we're all headed for.

> Earl Hamner, Jr., creator of *The Waltons*

FRED SANFORD: I still want to sow some wild oats.
LAMONT SANFORD: At your age, you don't have no wild oats—you got shredded wheat.

> *Sanford and Son*

I don't know anything that'll age a fellow faster than girls.

> Ward Cleaver, *Leave It to Beaver*

BUD ANDERSON: You've been around so long and seen so much and done so much, and still manage to look so good.
JIM ANDERSON: Thanks a lot!
BUD: I think you look real young. Honest. Younger than Joe Phillips' dad, younger than Claude Mesner's uncle, why even younger than—

JIM: Bud, before you have me back in kindergarten, see who's at the door, will you?

Father Knows Best

The Almighty

ARCHIE BUNKER: All the pictures I ever seen, God is white.
GEORGE JEFFERSON: Maybe you were looking at the negatives.

All in the Family

Alleviating Stress

Three. Two. One. One. Two. Three. What the heck is bothering me?

Carl Winslow, *Family Matters*

FRANK COSTANZA: The doctor gave me a relaxation cassette. When my blood pressure gets too high, the man on the tape tells me to say: "SERENITY NOW"
GEORGE COSTANZA: Are you supposed to yell it?
FRANK: The man on the tape wasn't specific.

Seinfeld

Allowances

HOMER SIMPSON: Well, these bills will have to be paid out of your allowance.

BART SIMPSON: You'll have to raise my allowance to about a thousand dollars a week.

HOMER: Then that's what I'll do, smart guy.

The Simpsons

America

There. Right there, Peg, is the problem with America. We've lost our spirit of self-reliance. Something's broken, call someone. Something's leaking, call someone. One of the kids suffers a ruptured appendix, call someone. Whatever happened to rugged American manhood?

Al Bundy, *Married . . . with Children*

You know, America is a great place, but it doesn't have a place where you can get rid of your kids.

Cliff Huxtable, *The Cosby Show*

The American Dream

GEORGE JEFFERSON: It's the American dream come true: Ten years ago, I was a little guy with one store. And now look at me . . .

LOUISE JEFFERSON: Now you're a little guy with seven stores.
The Jeffersons

This is America, where a right makes might, where justice is blind, where law is king, where a man should be able to pursue his democratic right no matter what it costs him in time, effort and/or money.
Fred Sanford, *Sanford and Son*

There's about three great moments in a man's life: when he buys a house, and a car, and a new color TV. That's what America is all about.
Archie Bunker, *All in the Family*

Kill my boss? Do I dare live out the American dream?
Homer Simpson, *The Simpsons*

The American Way

That ain't the American way, buddy. . . . You don't know nothin' about Lady Liberty standin' there with her torch on high screamin' out to all of the nations of the world. Send me your poor, your deadbeats, your filthy. And all them nations sent them in here—they came swarming like ants. Your Spanish PRs, your Japs, your Chinamen, your Krauts, and your England fags. All of 'em come to live here, and they're all free to live in their own separate sections where they feel safe and they'll bust your head if you go in there. That's what makes America great, buddy.

Archie Bunker, *All in the Family*

Lisa, if you don't like your job, you don't strike; you just go in every day and do it really half-assed—that's the American way.

Homer Simpson, *The Simpsons*

Anger

Dogs get mad. Human beings get angry.

Cliff Huxtable, *The Cosby Show*

Anniversaries

BARNEY FIFE: The last big buy was my mom and dad's anniversary present.

ANDY TAYLOR: What'd you get 'em?

BARNEY: A septic tank.

ANDY: For their anniversary?

BARNEY: They're awful hard to buy for. Besides, it was something they could use. They were really thrilled. It had two tons of concrete in it. All steel reinforced.

ANDY: You're a fine son, Barn.
BARNEY: I try.

The Andy Griffith Show

JAN BRADY: Do you think mom suspects anything?
MIKE BRADY: She suspects one thing.
JAN: What?
MIKE: That I'm a husband who forgets wedding anniversaries.

The Brady Bunch

Absolutely not. I have something very important planned for that day which requires total silence. I can't get too technical, but it involves your mother, our anniversary and not making love to her 'til I shrivel up and die. Now, if you don't mind, I am going to walk blindly in traffic.

Al Bundy, *Married . . . with Children*

Artistic Pursuits

Artists are always ready to sacrifice for art, if the price is right.

Gomez Addams, *The Addams Family*

You know, if Michelangelo had used me as a model, there's no telling how far he could have gone.

Herman Munster, *The Munsters*

The Average Guy

Everybody gets a crazy desire to be a regular person at some point in their life.

> Willy Lawrence, *Family*

Bachelorhood

CHIP DOUGLAS: What's a bachelor?
MIKE DOUGLAS: That's a man who thinks before he acts.
BUB O'CASEY: . . . And then doesn't act.

> *My Three Sons*

Bad Luck

It's bad luck to take advice from insane people.

> Herb Tarlek, *WKRP in Cincinnati*

Beer

All right, number one—if it wasn't for beer, there would be at least three people who probably wouldn't be married—me, Jefferson, and probably Lisa Marie Presley. Number two—since men buy beer, advertisers have to cater to what we want. And hold on to your corncob pipe—we like pretty women. Pretty women sell beer, ugly women sell tennis rackets. Pretty women—cars; ugly women—minivans. Pretty women make us buy beer, and ugly women make us drink beer.

Al Bundy, *Married . . . with Children*

HOMER SIMPSON: Okay, brain. You don't like me and I don't like you, but let's get through this thing, and then I can continue killing you with beer.
HOMER'S BRAIN: It's a deal.

The Simpsons

Being Cool

TOMMY SOLOMON: I'm now the coolest punk in school.
DICK SOLOMON: Well, congratulations. What did you do?
TOMMY: I got suspended for setting off the fire alarm.
DICK: They suspended you? You saved hundreds of lives.
TOMMY: That's the best part. There was no fire.
DICK: Tommy, this is outrageous. The next time you set off the fire alarm you damn well better start a fire first.

3rd Rock from the Sun

Being Fat

I love my blubber. It keeps me warm; it keeps me company; it keeps my pants up.

Oscar Madison, *The Odd Couple*

Being a Gentleman

There's no rule against being a gentleman at school.

    Ward Cleaver, *Leave It to Beaver*

Being a Good Samaritan

KRISTEN SHEPPARD: You want me to sell myself so I can spy on your friends. Is that it?

J.R. EWING: Well, you're always saying you want to help.

    Dallas

Remember, it's better to give—than to get five across your lips.

    Fred Sanford, *Sanford and Son*

Being a Man

WARD CLEAVER: You know, Wally, shaving is just one of the outward signs of being a man. It's more important to try to be a man inside first.

WALLY CLEAVER: Yeah sure, Dad.

    Leave It to Beaver

Well, in the words of Harry S. Truman, "If it's too hot in the kitchen, stay away from the cook."

    Archie Bunker, *All in the Family*

D.J. CONNER: I thought it was good to be a man.

DAN CONNER: Oh no, not since the 1960s.

Roseanne

LUKE SPENCER: You really freaked your mother out. Did it make you feel like a man?

LUCKY SPENCER: Did raping her make you feel like one?

General Hospital

Being Poor

FRED SANFORD: When I was a kid, we slept seven in one bed—same bed, same underwear. When I was a youngster, I wore one pair of tennis shoes five years—wore them up to the name on the ankle. Now that's poor.

Sanford and Son

GEORGE JEFFERSON: If I paid you to think, you could cash your check at the penny arcade.

FLORENCE JOHNSTON: Where do you think I cash it now?

The Jeffersons

We are poor, and poor is one of three things people don't want to be. Right next to sick and dead.

James Evans, *Good Times*

Being Responsible

A man does what he has to do—if he can't get out of it.
>Pappy Maverick, *Maverick*

Being Wrong

By George, it's not easy to admit you're wrong, but it's obviously the right thing to do.
>Jim Anderson, *Father Knows Best*

Best Friends

The best friend that a husband can ever possibly have should be his wife and vice versa.
>Tom Corbett, *The Courtship of Eddie's Father*

The Birds and the Bees

RITCHIE PETRIE: Daddy, where did I come from?
ROB PETRIE: Well, uh . . . let's see. Uh . . . where's Dr. Spock?
>*The Dick Van Dyke Show*

GRANNY: Elly May done popped the buttons off her shirt again.
JED CLAMPETT: Elly May carries herself proud with her shoulders throwed back.

GRANNY: It ain't her shoulders that have been poppin' these buttons.

The Beverly Hillbillies

MARION CUNNINGHAM: In California, they teach the kids the birds and the bees right in school.
HOWARD CUNNINGHAM: That's California, this is Milwaukee. The birds and the bees are only here four months out of the year.

Happy Days

RAY BARONE: It turned out that Allie didn't want the sex talk! She asked me why God put us on earth!
DEBRA BARONE: So, what did you tell her?
RAY: I told her heaven was too crowded . . . And then I faked a cold and got the hell out of there.

Everybody Loves Raymond

Birth Control

Birth control . . . don't do it.

Eric Foreman, *That '70s Show*

Booze

Alcohol, the cause of and solution to all life's problems.

Homer Simpson, *The Simpsons*

HOMER SIMPSON: This is it. The last bar in Springfield. If they don't let me in, I'll have to quit drinking.

HOMER'S LIVER: YAY.

HOMER: Shut up, liver . . .

The Simpsons

Bowling

(*On the phone with Jerry Springer*) Listen Jerry, bowling is a man's sport. If God had wanted women to bowl, he would have put their breasts on their backs so we would have something to watch while waiting our turn.

Al Bundy, *Married . . . with Children*

Breaking Up with a Woman

BUB O'CASEY: How do you go about unloading women?—in case I should ever have that problem.

CHIP DOUGLAS: It's real easy. All ya have to say is "thanks for the dance. I can't see you anymore 'cause I think you give me a rash."

My Three Sons

Cadillacs

There's more black men in white Cadillacs than white men in black Cadillacs.

Fred Sanford, *Sanford and Son*

Capital Punishment

It's a proven fact that capital punishment is a known detergent to crime.

Archie Bunker, *All in the Family*

Cars

I know I get crazy about cars, you know. My car, your car, anybody's car. But it's, like Bat Masterson said: "You can't get obsessed the way old people drive through water, if their servants are on fire."

Tim Taylor, *Home Improvement*

WALLY CLEAVER: Gee, Dad, how come you know so much about buying cars?
WARD CLEAVER: Well, Wally, as unbelievable as it may seem they did have cars in my younger days.
WALLY: Used cars?

Leave It to Beaver

Cats

I hate cats. They always look like they're keeping a secret and they know somethin' you don't. Plus they do their business in a box, and I'm telling ya, that's not right!

Victor Pellet, *In-Laws*

Celebrity Worship

GENE BERGMAN: Why are you so starstruck? In New York, we lived next door to the man who won the Nobel Prize in Physics.

ANNIE BERGMAN: Yeah, but I didn't lose my virginity listening to one of those lectures on the quantum theory.

Something Wilder

Charity

You can't expect a handout every time you want something.

Mike Brady, *The Brady Bunch*

I wouldn't give you the dust off my car.

J.R. Ewing, *Dallas*

When you give something and you get something in return, that's the best feeling in the world.

> Andy Taylor, *The Andy Griffith Show*

Child Rearing

FRED SANFORD: Didn't you learn anything being my son? Who do you think I did this for?
LAMONT SANFORD: Yourself.
FRED: Yeah, you learned something.

> *Sanford and Son*

JUNE CLEAVER: Dear, do you think all parents have this much trouble?
WARD CLEAVER: No, just parents with children.

> *Leave It to Beaver*

You can't raise a baby under a bowling alley.

> Danny Williams, *Make Room for Daddy*
> *(The Danny Thomas Show)*

Childish Pranks

Why can't you be a normal boy and swallow goldfish?

> Howard Cunningham, *Happy Days*

THEO HUXTABLE: Hey, dad. Am I really in that much trouble?

CLIFF HUXTABLE: Let me tell you something. Your mother and I could go into the kitchen. You can go out and get in MY car. You can drive BACKWARDS to Coney Island, run over the hot dog man and TWO stop signs, and you won't be in any more trouble than you are in now.

The Cosby Show

Child Psychology

STEVE DOUGLAS: Don't forget your promise. You be sure and say something nice to her.

BUB O'CASEY: That's using the old child psychology.

STEVE: Oh, sure. You tell 'em what to do and they do it.

My Three Sons

Christmas Spirit

Don't talk to me about Christmas, will ya? All that sticky, phony goodwill. I'd like to get a giant candy cane and beat the wings off a sugarplum fairy.

Oscar Madison, *The Odd Couple*

Edith, come on. "'Tis the season to be jolly," so be jolly.

Archie Bunker, *All in the Family*

Church

Edith, Sunday's supposed to be the day of rest. How can I rest when I'm going to church?

> Archie Bunker, *All in the Family*

Commercials

No intense offended there, but you know your voice doesn't, uh, insfire, the same amount of trust there as that dame that comes on after, you know, the one that advertises the spray for assisting the feminine hi-jinks.

> Archie Bunker, *All in the Family*

Conscience

A conscience is like a boat or a car. If you feel you need one, rent it.

> J.R. Ewing, *Dallas*

You should always listen to your conscience—that little voice that tells you you're doing the right thing.

> Carl Winslow, *Family Matters*

ARCHIE BUNKER: My conscience don't talk to me.
GLORIA STIVIC: I don't blame it. It shouldn't talk to strangers.

> *All in the Family*

The Constitution

The Constitution of the United States, for instance, is a marvelous document for self-government by the Christian people. But the minute you turn the document into the hands of non-Christian people and atheistic people they can use it to destroy the very foundation of our society. And that's what's been happening.

Pat Robertson, *700 Club*

Corporal Punishment

When will you people learn? In America we stopped using corporal punishment and things have never been better. The streets are safe, old people strut confidently through the darkest alleys, and the weak and nerdy are admired for their computer programming abilities. So, like us, let your children run wild and free, for as the Bible tells us, "Let your children run wild and free."

Homer Simpson, *The Simpsons*

The Cost of Raising Kids

Well, according to my research, the cost of raising a baby from birth to college is approximately seven hundred and eighty thousand dollars. Thanks to my actually selling a shoe last week, I'm proud to say we're now just short seven hundred eighty thousand dollars. Thank you.

Al Bundy, *Married . . . with Children*

Courtroom Etiquette

A husband can't testify against his wife.

Mike Brady, *The Brady Bunch*

Crooks

Once a crook, always a crook.

James Evans, *Good Times*

You know something? Call it a hunch, but I think Lou's a crook. I can't believe the nerve of that guy. He came to me looking for a job because he couldn't get one on account of his prison record. I said, "Hey, how about handling my money?" And he turns right around and steals from me. I don't know, maybe I just can't read people.

Edward Stratton, *Silver Spoons*

Croquet

Now, if you'll observe, my dear, croquet is a combination of two things: Balance, timing, superb coordination and a killer's instinct.

> Gomez Addams, *The Addams Family*

Cuddling

Men don't like to cuddle. We only like it if it leads to . . . you know . . . lower cuddling.

> Ray Barone, *Everybody Loves Raymond*

Curfews

DAN CONNER: I don't care what your story is. The rule is: you call.

DARLENE CONNER: It was a bad neighborhood. When I finally found a phone booth I got tired of waiting for the guy in it to finish peeing.

> *Roseanne*

PHILLIP BANKS: You're grounded for ten years.

ASHLEY BANKS: What? But that's not fair.

PHILLIP: Tell it to the judge . . . Oh yeah. That's me.

ASHLEY: It's still not fair. The Menendez brothers are going to be free before I am.

PHILLIP: That's because the Menendez Brothers got home on time.

> *Fresh Prince of Bel-Air*

Dancing

When I dance, people think I'm looking for my keys.

Ray Barone, *Everybody Loves Raymond*

Dating

As long as it's okay with my daughter. Otherwise, you will continue to date her and no one but her, until she is finished with you. Because if you make her cry, I will make you cry.

Paul Hennessy, *8 Simple Rules . . . for Dating My Teenage Daughter*

CISSY: Uncle Bill, this is Ronnie. We decided to go steady.
UNCLE BILL: Just what does "going steady" mean nowadays?
CISSY: It means that Ronnie and I will only date each other, then in a couple of years think about getting married.

Family Affair

You date one woman all the time and pretty soon people start taking you for granted. They don't say "let's invite Andy" or "let's invite Ellie." No, they say "let's invite Andy and Ellie." And then that's when a woman gets her claws into you.

Andy Taylor, *The Andy Griffith Show*

Kyle, just so you know: If you ever pull into my driveway and honk, you better be delivering a package because you're sure as hell not picking anything up.

> Paul Hennessy, *8 Simple Rules . . . for Dating My Teenage Daughter*

Daughters

You know, one of these days daughters may go out of style. Fathers won't be able to afford them.

> Jim Anderson, *Father Knows Best*

Death

Everybody's scared o' death 'til it hits you. After that, you don't give it a second thought.

> Archie Bunker, *All in the Family*

Anybody who would die for a practical joke deserves to get his laugh.

> Rob Petrie, *The Dick Van Dyke Show*

When I die it ain't gonna be from nothin' serious.

> Archie Bunker, *All in the Family*

Oh Bart, don't worry, people die all the time. In fact, you could wake up dead tomorrow.

Homer Simpson, *The Simpsons*

Debt

I've got a wife, two kids, and ten finance companies to support. How am I supposed to pay my bills?

George Jetson, *The Jetsons*

Demanding Spouses

Roseanne and *demand*. Two words that go together like waffle iron and forehead.

Dan Conner, *Roseanne*

Democracy

What's the point of having democracy if everybody's going to vote wrong?

Dick Solomon, *3rd Rock from the Sun*

Dieting

God did not give man a belly just to hang a button on.

Archie Bunker, *All in the Family*

KATIE KANISKY: Dad, it's hard for Nell to stick to her diet when you're stuffing your face.

CHIEF CARL KANISKY: I'm not stuffing my face.

NELL HARPER: Right. He's eating for two in case he gets pregnant.

CHIEF: See what happens? You take away their trough and they get vicious.

NELL: It's no problem. I'm eating clean, lean, and healthy. After all, you are what you eat. Another helping of jackass, chief?

Gimme a Break!

Dinner Reservations

WALLY CLEAVER: There's no trick to it, is there?

WARD CLEAVER: No, you just speak up, tell them you want a table for two and tell them when.

Leave It to Beaver

Disappointment

Sometimes when you make a deal and it turns out badly, the best thing you can do is get out of it.

Mike Brady, *The Brady Bunch*

Discipline

You have to keep a firm hand on boys nowadays. My boy Clarence answered me back the other day and I smacked him. None of that psychology stuff for me.

Fred Rutherford, *Leave It to Beaver*

You know, the toughest thing is to love somebody who has done something mean to you. Especially when that somebody has been yourself. Have you ever done anything mean to yourself? Well, it's very important to look inside yourself and find that loving part of you. That's the part that you must take good care of and *never* be mean to. Because that's the part of you that allows you to love your neighbor. And your neighbor is anyone you happen to be with at any time in your life. Respecting and loving your neighbor can give everybody a good feeling.

Fred Rogers, *Mister Rogers' Neighborhood*

Dreams

Dad had one great dream, a dream that had been handed down from generation to generation of male Bundys: to build their own room and live separately from their wives. Sadly, they all failed.

Al Bundy, *Married . . . with Children*

Dreaming Through Your Children

JAMES EVANS: I want to give him something better than I got when I turned eighteen.

FLORIDA EVANS: What was that?

JAMES: A draft notice.

Good Times

WARD CLEAVER: Beaver, parents have their share too. As you grow older you come to realize that some of the ambitions and dreams you had are just not going to come true, so you begin to dream through your children.

WALLY CLEAVER: You mean Mr. Rutherford dreams through Lumpy?

Leave It to Beaver

Dressing for Success

STEVEN KEATON: Alex, you're a young man. You shouldn't be worried about success. You should be thinking about hopping on a tramp steamer and going around the world, or putting a pack on your back and heading down to Mexico or South America or anywhere.

ALEX KEATON: The sixties are over, Dad.

STEVEN: Thanks for the tip.

Family Ties

Driving

Maybe when a husband and wife change places in a car, it upsets the cosmic order of things.

Jim Anderson, *Father Knows Best*

Drugs

Let me tell you something. You know how I feel and how your mother feels about drugs. Now, as long as you're living in this house, you are not to do drugs. When you move into your own house, you are not to do any drugs. When I am dead and you are seventy-five, you are not to do any drugs.

Cliff Huxtable, *The Cosby Show*

HANK HILL: Bobby, promise me you won't do drugs. Promise me.
BOBBY HILL: I promise.
HANK: Promises mean nothing.
BOBBY: Look, Dad, I'm not gonna do drugs. I want to be the first chubby comedian to live past thirty-five.

King of the Hill

Dude, we have known about your dope problem for a long while now, I mean, don't you think I know what it means when you phone for a pizza at twelve o'clock at night?

Ozzy Osbourne, *The Osbournes*

DARLENE CONNER: Oh come on, Dad, do you really think what I did was that bad?

DAN CONNER: Yes.

DARLENE: Give me a break. You grew up in the sixties. I've seen the photo album. I mean, those clothes had to have some pharmaceutical explanation.

> *Roseanne*

Eating

My baloney has a first name, it's H-O-M-E-R, my baloney has a second name, it's H-O-M-E-R.

> Homer Simpson, *The Simpsons*

You boys better get washed up—it's almost time for lunch.

> Ward Cleaver, *Leave It to Beaver*

BECKY CONNER: No one could eat this crud.

DAN CONNER: Hey, if you don't finish your crud, you're not gonna get any crap for dessert.

> *Roseanne*

Nobody could dial a breakfast like mother.

> George Jetson, *The Jetsons*

FLORENCE JOHNSTON: Is there something you don't like about my cooking?

GEORGE JEFFERSON: Yeah—eating it.

The Jeffersons

PHILLIP BANKS: Geoffrey, bring me my tools.

GEOFFREY: Do you mean your knife and fork, sir?

The Fresh Prince of Bel-Air

AUNT BEA: Did you like the white beans?

ANDY TAYLOR: Uh huh.

AUNT BEA: Well, you didn't say anything.

ANDY: Well, I ate four bowls. If that ain't a tribute to white beans, I don't know what is.

AUNT BEA: Well . . .

ANDY: Eating speaks louder than words.

AUNT BEA: You know, your education was worth every penny of it.

The Andy Griffith Show

You boys better get washed. It's time for supper.

Ward Cleaver, *Leave It to Beaver*

GUARDIAN: Hog jowls, possum pie! Do you intend to feed those things to Master Armstrong?

JED CLAMPETT: Why? Don't he eat that good at home?

The Beverly Hillbillies

DICK SOLOMON: Mary, the waiter made a mistake. You ordered the Surf and Turf. They brought you the steak and lobster.

3rd Rock from the Sun

JOANIE CUNNINGHAM: Barbara Jo Allen ate a fly.
HOWARD CUNNINGHAM: Well, with beef at sixty-eight cents a pound, I don't blame her.

Happy Days

FRED SANFORD: We could have a little pork and beans now and a little zucchini later. Or a little zucchini now and a little pork and beans later. Or if you like the pork and beans, you can have them and I'll take the zucchini, or I can take the pork and beans and you take the zucchini. So what will it be? Zucchini or pork and beans?

Sanford and Son

Eating cardboard can ruin your life. You could end up in the street living in a box. Then you'll eat the box, and you'll be homeless.

Dan Conner, *Roseanne*

One wonderful way of showing that you love people is being able to accept the food they give you. If you really like it and you can tell them so, that can give them a very, very good feeling.

I think of these television visits as my way of giving to you. I'm glad that you like to be with us. Bye-bye.

Fred Rogers, *Mister Rogers' Neighborhood*

(*Praying*) Dear Lord, the gods have been good to me. As an offering, I present these milk and cookies. If you wish me to eat them instead, please give me no sign whatsoever. (*brief pause*) Thy bidding will be done. (*munch munch munch*)

Homer Simpson, *The Simpsons*

You better get washed up, boys. It's almost time for dinner.

Ward Cleaver, *Leave It to Beaver*

Eavesdropping

BEAVER CLEAVER: But dad said you wouldn't do it.
WARD CLEAVER: Beaver, were you eavesdropping again?
BEAVER: Oh no, dad. I was just listening.

Leave It To Beaver

Education

ADAM CARTWRIGHT: Education is progress. Now what have you got against it?
BEN: I don't have anything against it—as long as it doesn't interfere with your thinking.

Bonanza

COACH HAYDEN FOX: You graduated from college and now you
   won't wash my car?
DAUBER: Uh huh.
COACH FOX: You see, this is why I hate education.
   Coach

The public education movement has also been an anti-Christian
movement. We can change education in America if you put
Christian principles in and Christian pedagogy in. In three
years, you would totally revolutionize education in America.
   Pat Robertson, *700 Club*

Woo-hoo! Who woulda guessed reading and writing would pay
off?
   Homer Simpson, *The Simpsons*

Effort

If you're going to do something, you've got to give it all you've
got.
   Mike Brady, *The Brady Bunch*

Kids, you tried your best and you failed miserably. The lesson
is, never try.
   Homer Simpson, *The Simpsons*

Embarrassment

You wanna put your mother and me through the same kind of shame? Besmooze the family name like that?

> Archie Bunker, *All in the Family*

Maybe, just once, someone will call me "sir" without adding "you're making a scene."

> Homer Simpson, *The Simpsons*

The Empty Nest

Once my kids finally leave the house, I'll finally be able to do what every man is supposed to. I can watch TV. I can . . . Well, I don't know, but it doesn't matter. It's still better than having a screaming, crapping, money-sucking little vampire bobsledding me to the graveyard. God I feel good.

> Al Bundy, *Married . . . with Children*

Equal Rights

MICHAEL EVANS: I won't rest until our people have everything the whites have.
FLORIDA EVANS: We've already got it. Unemployment. Inflation. Taxation. Aggravation.

JAMES EVANS: You're right, baby. When it comes to misery they sure gave us equal rights.

Good Times

Ex-Wives

RICKY STRATTON: I've always tried to imagine what you look like, but whenever I asked mom she just showed me a picture of a horse's rear end.

EDWARD STRATTON: Now, see the temptation here would be to insult your mother back, but I like to think that I'm bigger than that. She's over thirty now—that's over two hundred and ten in dog years.

Silver Spoons

Faith

Faith is something that you believe that nobody in their right mind would believe.

Archie Bunker, *All in the Family*

Family

All of us hope to ease the pain of a loved one, even though that's almost impossible. You know, you gave life—you and

Libby—to Mary Ellen in there and pain is very much a part of life.

> Grandpa "Zeb" Walton, *The Waltons*

Whatever trouble he's in, his family has a right to share it with him. It's our duty to help him if we can and it's his duty to let us and he doesn't have the privilege to share that.

> Jarrord Barkley, *The Big Valley*

The first rule of orphanages and Irish families is there's always room for one more.

> Father Francis Mulcahy, *M*A*S*H*

If you're gonna steal from kin—at least they're less likely to put the law on you.

> Bret Maverick, *Maverick*

We're a family and a family is only as strong as the glue that holds that family together. As an architect, I've learned a lesson that a house isn't just made of fake wood paneling, shag carpet, and Formica. As long as the glue that holds that house together is strong that's all that matters.

> Mike Brady, *A Very Brady Sequel*

Listen to me, the only reason I did this is because you're my nephew, and I love you. If it were anybody else, they would've gotten that intervention through the back of their f***ing head.

Tony Soprano, *The Sopranos*

Fantasies

Al is living every guy's fantasy . . . every *single* guy's fantasy. Married guys don't have fantasies; they're taken away from them. Er, it's a good thing, because then you get to, you know, give all your attention to your wife. You know, year after year. Month in, month out. Day after day after day until you're dead.

Tim Taylor, *Home Improvement*

Marge, you're my wife and I love you very much. But you're living in a world of make-believe. With flowers and bells and leprechauns, and magic frogs with funny little hats.

Homer Simpson, *The Simpsons*

Fathers

I am your father. I brought you in this world, and I'll take you out.

Cliff Huxtable, *The Cosby Show*

Don't forget: your dad is your best friend.

> Theme song from *The Courtship of Eddie's Father*

Being a father is something that lives in your heart and grows over a long period of time.

> Starman, *Starman*

Well, I suppose Father knows best.

> Margaret Anderson, *Father Knows Best*

Daddies make the best friends. Why do you think dogs always hang around with them?

> Cliff Huxtable, *The Cosby Show*

Fathers and Sons

There are no rules for fathers and sons.

> Andy Taylor, *The Andy Griffith Show*

Feelings

The thing to do when you're feeling sad is to shoot for the good feelings.

> Andy Taylor, *The Andy Griffith Show*

Only you know what you're thinking and feeling. Those are all things you can talk about with the people you love. It's important to talk.

Fred Rogers, *Mister Rogers' Neighborhood*

Females

There can't be such a thing as the female eunuch because the what-you-gotta-have to get that a woman ain't got in the first place.

Archie Bunker, *All in the Family*

TIM TAYLOR: A woman? You brought me here to see a woman?

JILL TAYLOR: I didn't know she was a woman. My gynecologist just said Dr. Kaplan was the best urologist in town.

TIM: How am I supposed to talk to a woman about what's going on in Manland?

JILL: "Manland"? Now you got a theme park between your legs?

Home Improvement

JETHRO BODINE: Uncle Jed, she handed me a big old sugar cookie, looked at me and said, "Jethro, if you had a choice between that cookie and me, which one would you take?" Uncle Jed, that's when I found out just how fast she was. I had to run nearly a mile to get away from her with that cookie.

JED CLAMPETT: Jethro, someday me and you gotta have a long talk.

The Beverly Hillbillies

Fighting

Fighting isn't the answer to anything. If it were, the biggest and the strongest would always be right.

Mike Brady, *The Brady Bunch*

Your mother and I have our differences once in a while, but we don't settle them by throwing furniture at each other.

Jim Anderson, *Father Knows Best*

First Dates

FELIX UNGER: When I took her home, I didn't try to kiss her or anything like that. I was a perfect gentleman. I've never forgotten it.
OSCAR MADISON: I'll bet she did.

The Odd Couple

The First Day of School

No more of our children's friends going through our refrigerator like locusts and leaving us with nothing but a box of Arm & Hammer.

Cliff Huxtable, *The Cosby Show*

Flattery

(*To wife, Sue Ellen*) Don't flatter yourself, honey. You're just another Ewing possession. Like an oil lease, you're easily disposable.

J.R. Ewing, *Dallas*

The Flintstones

If the Flintstones have taught us anything, it's that pelicans can be used to mix cement.

Homer Simpson, *The Simpsons*

Flu

Roseanne, I've got bad stuff coming out of every opening.

Dan Conner, *Roseanne*

Folk Music

STEVEN KEATON: Hey, what are you doing? I was listening to that.

ALEX KEATON: That's depressing, Dad. This is an up night. This guy sounds like he's in pain.

STEVEN: He's supposed to be in pain. He's a folk singer.

Family Ties

Foosball

There's nothing better than a nice chat over a rousing game of foosball.

Edward Stratton, *Silver Spoons*

Football

He's a football player, and football players know how to treat a woman right.

Hank Hill, *King of the Hill*

For Michigan fans, football is a religion. And the Ohio State game is Easter.

Paul Hennessy, *8 Simple Rules . . . for Dating My Teenage Daughter*

Forgiveness

Sometimes when someone makes a mistake and does something wrong, that's when they need understanding the most.

Ward Cleaver, *Leave It to Beaver*

Foul Language

Hey, the language! Do you blow your father with that mouth?

Tony Soprano, *The Sopranos*

Funerals

Funerals are all the same—nothing's ever different—except for the dearly departed.

Archie Bunker, *All in the Family*

Geography

CHIP DOUGLAS: Dad, where are the Azores?
STEVE DOUGLAS: Probably right where you threw 'em.
CHIP: Isn't the ocean someplace a good enough answer?
STEVE: Well, that's a good start, but why don't you take a look
and see if they still aren't around Portugal somewhere.

My Three Sons

JENNIFER KEATON: Anybody know what the capital of Iowa is?

STEVEN KEATON: Iowa is the one state that has no capital, so you see it is the responsibility of every American to look after Iowa.

Family Ties

Getting Drunk

RICHIE CUNNINGHAM: All we had was beer in teeny-weenie little glasses.

HOWARD CUNNINGHAM: How many teeny-weeny glasses did you have?

RICHIE: Seventy-two.

Happy Days

MEL SHARPLES: People drink because it makes 'em feel good.

TOMMY HYATT: Is that how you feel now?

MEL: I just had a little too much good.

Alice

LOIS GRIFFIN: You're drunk again.

PETER GRIFFIN: No, I'm just exhausted 'cause I've been up all night drinking.

Family Guy

Getting Fired

They said if I came in late again that I would get fired, and I can't risk that, so I'm not going.

Homer Simpson, *The Simpsons*

Gifts

A gift is only a good thing when the giver has given thought to that gift. But when the gift the giver gives gives grief then that gift should give the giver regrets.

Mike Brady, *A Very Brady Sequel*

I'm gonna come back with the best gift a husband can get a wife—an annulment from my second wife.

Homer Simpson, *The Simpsons*

Gilligan's Island

MIKE SEAVER: *Gilligan's Island* is on every day at three-thirty . . . whether I watch it or not.
JASON SEAVER: What's the point?
MIKE: Dad, it's not for me. It's just—on.

Growing Pains

Giving In

KIMBERLY DRUMMOND: Thanks, Dad. You're terrific.
PHILLIP DRUMMOND: Yeah, I'm always terrific when I cave in.
   Diff'rent Strokes

The Gold Rush

The Gold Rush was over, gone like a soap bubble in the sun. The Ponderosa was just as it has always been. And we went home.

   Ben Cartwright, *Bonanza*

Golf

JED CLAMPETT: We're going to be shooting some game called "golf."
GRANNY: What in tarnation is a "golf."
JED: I don't know, but they must be thicker'n crows in a corn patch around here because everybody in Beverly Hills shoots 'em.

   The Beverly Hillbillies

Going Out

What's the point of going out? We're just going to wind up back here anyway.

Homer Simpson, *The Simpsons*

Good Deeds

A good deed is sufficient unto itself.

Ward Cleaver, *Leave It to Beaver*

The Good Old Days

Son, I wish you could've been around when I was younger. Of course, I probably wouldn't have let you hang out with me.

Al Bundy, *Married . . . with Children*

That's another thing. I don't want to hear anymore how it was in your day. From now on, keep your anecdotes to local color, like Dinoflow or the Maguire sisters. Otherwise, SHUT THE F *** UP!

Tony Soprano, *The Sopranos*

I've gone back in time to when dinosaurs weren't just confined to zoos.

Homer Simpson, *The Simpsons*

Goodbyes

MIKE STIVIC: You've been like a father to me.
ARCHIE BUNKER: Well, you've been just like a son to me. You never did nothin' I ever told you to do.

All in the Family

Greed

WILLIE TANNER: Some people are so blinded by the thirst for money that it causes them to lose their values and do things they shouldn't do.
ALF: Well, that explains *Ghostbusters II*.

Alf

Growing Up

GREG BRADY: Why didn't you stop me, Dad?
MIKE BRADY: Because I believe you just proved you're old enough to stop yourself.

The Brady Bunch

Well, if he's worried about buttons on his clothes it's a sure sign he's growing up.

> Ward Cleaver, *Leave It to Beaver*

Guns

Guns don't kill people. Physics kills people.

> Dick Solomon, *3rd Rock from the Sun*

If I had time to clean up the mess, I'd shoot you.

> J.R. Ewing, *Dallas*

Whoever invented guns ought to be shot.

> George Jefferson, *The Jeffersons*

David, there are two and a half million dollars' worth of toys in this house. Why do you always have to play with the gun?

> Detective Barney Miller, *Barney Miller*

DAN CONNER: Have you considered getting a gun for the diner?
ROSEANNE CONNER: Oh, there's a great idea. A loaded gun in the same room as my mother and my sister! What if they miss each other and kill a customer?
DAN: Then they'll have to reload.

> *Roseanne*

BOBBY HILL: Can I put a gun rack on my bike?
HANK HILL: Do you know how long I've been waiting for you to ask that?

> *King of the Hill*

When I held that gun in my hand, I felt a surge of power . . . like God must feel when he's holding a gun.

> Homer Simpson, *The Simpsons*

I feel that if a gun is good enough to protect something as important as a bar, then it's good enough to protect my family.

> Homer Simpson, *The Simpsons*

Gun Control

GLORIA STIVIC: Did you know that sixty-five percent of the people murdered in this country were killed by handguns?
ARCHIE BUNKER: Would it make you feel any better, little girl, if they was pushed out of windows?

> *All in the Family*

Hair

TIM TAYLOR: You look like an idiot. I don't understand. None of your friends have haircuts like this.

BRAD TAYLOR: Well, you're the one who's always telling me not to be like my friends. I mean, if all my friends jumped in the lake would you want me to?

TIM: If they were like this, I'd ask you to join in.

Home Improvement

Halloween

I think we ought to close Halloween down. Do you want your children to dress up as witches? The Druids used to dress up like this when they were doing human sacrifice. [Your children] are acting out Satanic rituals and participating in it, and don't even realize it.

Pat Robertson, *700 Club*

Why don't we just call it what it is: begging!

Cliff Huxtable, *The Cosby Show*

LITTLE GIRL: Trick or Treat! I'm an angel!

PAUL HENNESSY: Yeah, you may be an angel now, but in a few years you're going to be killing your father!

8 Simple Rules . . . for Dating My Teenage Daughter

Heart Attacks

OPAL COURTLAND: You could have another heart attack if you're aggravated enough.
PALMER COURTLAND: Then leave. Save my life.

All My Children

Women don't get heart attacks. They give 'em.

Dwayne F. Schneider, *One Day at a Time*

Hell

LIZA CHANDLER: I'll tell you what: Go to hell.
ADAM CHANDLER: I'm already here, sweetheart. You're it.

All My Children

Heroes

Boys don't have many heroes they can look up to these days. If I let Eddie down, all he has left is Smokey the Bear.

Herman Munster, *The Munsters*

History

Look, all I know is that Columbus discovered Ohio in 1776.

Ricky Ricardo, *I Love Lucy*

Home

Our house is more important than money. This neighborhood is more important than money. We know so much about each other. I know that every January, Mr. Yeager is going to have that big Super Bowl party at his house. We know that at ten fifteen every Saturday morning, Mrs. Topping likes to walk through her living room naked. Call me old-fashioned, but these things are important, and they're not for sale.

Mike Brady, *The Brady Bunch Movie*

JED CLAMPETT: Pearl, what d'ya think? Think I ought to move?
COUSIN PEARL: Jed, how can ya even ask? Look around ya. You're eight miles from your nearest neighbor. You're overrun with skunks, possums, coyotes, bobcats. You use kerosene lamps for light, and you cook on a wood stove summer and winter. You're drinkin' homemade moonshine and washin' with lye soap. And you ask, "should I move?"
JED: I reckon you're right. A man'd be a dang fool to leave all this!

The Beverly Hillbillies

Ah, home sweet hell.

Al Bundy, *Married . . . with Children*

What a picture of domestic tranquility ... Hemlock on the hearth and my wife feeding the piranha.

Gomez Addams, *The Addams Family*

Homophobia

Little boys who play with dolls grow up to be other boys' roommates.

Archie Bunker, *All in the Family*

PAUL: Every person knows that *Homo sapiens* is a killer.
EDITH BUNKER: *Homo sapiens*. Is he an Arab?
ARCHIE: No, Edith. *Homo sapiens*. That's a killer fag.

All in the Family

(*About Gay Day at Disney World*) I would warn Orlando that you're right in the way of some serious hurricanes, and I don't think I'd be waving those flags in God's face if I were you. This is not a message of hate; this is a message of redemption. But a condition like this will bring about the destruction of your nation. It'll bring about terrorist bombs, it'll bring earthquakes, tornadoes, and possibly a meteor.

Pat Robertson, *700 Club*

I like my beer cold, my TV loud, and my homosexuals fa-laaaaming.

Homer Simpson, *The Simpsons*

Bobby, I know we've never talked about it, but someday I'm going to die. And on that day, you can go to cooking school.

Hank Hill, *King of the Hill*

ROSEANNE CONNER: Hey, Dan, if you're still gay, I could go for a Mimosa and some Eggs Florentine.
DAN CONNER: I don't cook for you. I'm Fred's bitch.

Roseanne

I am absolutely persuaded one of the reasons so many lesbians are at the forefront of the pro-choice movement is because being a mother is the unique characteristic of womanhood, and these lesbians will never be mothers naturally, so they don't want anybody else to have that privilege either.

Pat Robertson, *700 Club*

Honesty

You're honest and you expect others to be. That's a good philosophy, but don't always depend on it.

Jim Anderson, *Father Knows Best*

Houseguests

A guest is a guest, but a relative is a pest.

George Jefferson, *The Jeffersons*

Housekeepers

GEORGE JEFFERSON: She's what you call a domestic.
LOUISE JEFFERSON: You make it sound like a disease!
> *The Jeffersons*

Human Nature

I'm only human, Meathead . . . and to be human is to be violent.
> Archie Bunker, *All in the Family*

KRISTEN SHEPPARD: Familiarity breeds contempt, is that what you're saying?
J.R. EWING: Oh, I wouldn't say contempt exactly . . . But it does take some of the bloom off the rose, don't you think?
> *Dallas*

Weaseling out of things is important to learn. It's what separates us from the animals . . . except the weasel.
> Homer Simpson, *The Simpsons*

STEVEN KEATON: Alex, parents are conditioned to put up with a few minor accidents when they leave their children home alone. A broken vase, spilled milk on the rug . . . There was a kangaroo . . . in my living room.

ALEX KEATON: He was just here for the party, Dad.
STEVEN: Then I guess I'm overreacting.

> *Family Ties*

GRANDPA MUNSTER: Hmm. What smells so good?
HERMAN MUNSTER: I cut myself shaving.

> *The Munsters*

There's nothing more treacherous than an unemployed cobra.

> Uncle Joe Carson, *Petticoat Junction*

Hunger

Man, I'm hungry. As my old Texas grandfather used to say, "I could eat the horse and chase the rider."

> Jim Anderson, *Father Knows Best*

Ideals

Boy, it's easy to write about an ideal, but when it comes time to living it there sure are a lot of pitfalls.

> Tom Corbett, *The Courtship of Eddie's Father*

If I Was President

You know what I would do if I was president? I'd take a big empty state, that nobody's using—y'know, like Idaho—and I'd pack every pregnant woman in the country into doughnut trucks and convoy 'em all to Boise. And since Idaho means nothing anyhow, I'd change the name to Preg-naho.

Al Bundy, *Married . . . with Children*

I Love Lucy

Well, I hate Lucy. The real star was Fred. They should've killed off Ethel, Lucy, and that illegal alien . . . made Fred a single man and called it "Mertz's World," but . . . oh, well.

Al Bundy, *Married . . . with Children*

Imagination

I was just thinking: You know, if you had all the toys in the world and you didn't have any imagination about how you would play with them, those toys would just sit there doing nothing. And that would be no fun. Thinking up good things to do with what you have gives everybody a good feeling.

Fred Rogers, *Mister Rogers' Neighborhood*

Independence

No man is completely independent. No matter how big he may be, he still has to rely on other people.

Jim Anderson, *Father Knows Best*

Instruction Manuals

Okay, I know it looks complicated, but believe me, everything I need to know is right here in this seventy-five-page booklet—uh, much of it in English.

Dave Barry, *Dave's World*

Real men don't use instructions, son. Besides, this is just the manufacturer's opinion of how to put this together.

Tim Taylor, *Home Improvement*

Insults

AUNT ESTHER: Who you calling Ugly, Sucka?
FRED SANFORD: I'm calling you ugly. You so ugly I could stick your face into some dough and make some gorilla cookies.

Sanford and Son

All you got to do is enlist Esther in the Navy. And that way, you can have her face buried at sea!

    Fred Sanford, *Sanford and Son*

AUNT ESTHER: I've been blessed by Mother Nature!
FRED SANFORD: And when you got older, your face was cursed by Father Time.

    Sanford and Son

AUNT ESTHER: Fred Sanford, the wrath of God will strike you down.
FRED SANFORD: And this Louisville Slugger will knock you out.

    Sanford and Son

PALMER COURTLAND: Opal, you're one to talk. You really are. First of all, you consorted with drug dealers, and then you got arrested for assaulting one of them.
OPAL COURTLAND: Has your memory receded along with your hairline?

    All My Children

Italian Sayings

There's an old Italian saying: "You f**k up once, you lose two teeth."

    Tony Soprano, *The Sopranos*

Jealousy

I wasn't jealous, I was just upset that you were spending more time with that guy than you were with me, and I wanted to spend that time with you. Jealousy had nothing to do with it.

  Hank Hill, *King of the Hill*

Boy, you and Niles. It's been the same since you were kids. If one of you has something, the other one always has to have it too. I had to buy two Balinese lutes, two decoupage kits, two pairs of lederhosen. When you finally moved out of the house that was one embarrassing garage sale.

  Martin Crane, *Frasier*

Job Descriptions

I sell propane and propane accessories.

  Hank Hill, *King of the Hill*

I'm in the waste management business. Everybody immediately assumes you're mobbed up. It's a stereotype. And it's offensive. And you're the last person I would want to perpetuate it.

  Tony Soprano, *The Sopranos*

Jogging

Never go jogging in new underwear.

Carl Winslow, *Family Matters*

The Judicial System

GOMEZ ADDAMS: I've gone through the city ordinances, the Bill of Rights, and the seventeen volumes of assorted jurisprudence—and I've come to a conclusion.
MORTICIA ADDAMS: What?
GOMEZ: That we haven't got a leg to stand on.
UNCLE FESTER: Not even if we bribe the judge?

The Addams Family

JIM ANDERSON: Going to court isn't something to be ashamed of.
KATHY ANDERSON: Heck no, judges go all the time.

Father Knows Best

The courts are merely a ruse, if you will, for humanist, atheistic educators to beat up on Christians.

Pat Robertson, *700 Club*

Lawyers

I don't need no lawyer, I've already been robbed.
> Archie Bunker, *All in the Family*

Don't play lawyer-ball, son.
> Hank Hill, *King of the Hill*

I'm a gynecologist, and you want to talk to a lawyer?
> Cliff Huxtable, *The Cosby Show*

Leadership

JIM ANDERSON: Take the initiative. Be a leader.
BUD ANDERSON: Why does everybody have to be a leader? Why can't a guy just be a happy slob?
> *Father Knows Best*

I don't have any leadership qualities. . . . In high school I was president of the German Club; nobody would listen to me. If you can't get Germans to follow orders, who will?
> Felix Unger, *The Odd Couple*

Lessons to Live By

HOWARD CUNNINGHAM: You know, there's a lesson to be learned in all of this.
RICHIE CUNNINGHAM: I figured with all this embarrassment, there had to be a lesson in there somewhere.

Happy Days

When you want something done, go to the busy man. He's the one who'll find time to do it.

Jim Anderson, *Father Knows Best*

Never lose your passion, and don't forget your keys.

Steven Keaton, *Father Knows Best*

Anything worth having is worth going for all the way.

J.R. Ewing, *Dallas*

You can't take a step forward with both feet on the ground.

Mike Brady, *The Brady Bunch*

You want to know the meaning of life? You're born, you go to school, you go to work, you die. Marie . . . Cannoli!

Frank Barone, *Everyone Loves Raymond*

Don't forgive and never forget; do unto others before they do unto you; and third, and most importantly, keep your eye on your friends, because your enemies will take care of themselves.

J.R. Ewing, *Dallas*

Man does not live by milk alone.

Alex Stone, *The Donna Reed Show*

Well you know the old saying, son: "Uneasy lies the head that wears the crown."

Jim Anderson, *Father Knows Best*

A wrong decision is better than indecision.

Tony Soprano, *The Sopranos*

Lethargy

FRED FLINTSTONE: Where's your get up and go?
BARNEY RUBBLE: It just got up and went.

The Flintstones

Letting Go

Relinquishing responsibility to your kids is very hard for parents. You want to keep them safe, you want them to grow, but then you want to keep them as your little boy or your little girl forever. So basically I think you just tie them up and have a dungeon.

> Paul Hennessy, *8 Simple Rules . . . for Dating My Teenage Daughter*

ALEX KEATON: You really humiliated me, Dad. How could you do that?

STEVEN KEATON: It's hard to know when to interfere and when to let you go on your own. The line between protecting and interfering can get blurry. I tripped over it tonight, as you may have noticed.

> *Family Ties*

The Liberty Bell

The Liberty Bell is great. But if it was in a contest with a bunch of other bells *without* cracks, it would lose.

> Hank Hill, *King of the Hill*

Life Itself

BEAVER CLEAVER: Gee, there's something wrong with just about everything, isn't there, Dad?

WARD CLEAVER: Just about, Beav.

> *Leave It to Beaver*

WEDNESDAY ADDAMS: It's a black widow spider village.
GOMEZ ADDAMS: Amazing, just like a tiny human world.
WEDNESDAY: Yes, all they do is fight.
MORTICIA ADDAMS: Well, that's life.

> *The Addams Family*

You know, life's a real bumpy road. What you've got to develop are good shock absorbers.

> Uncle Charlie, *My Three Sons*

It's a fact of life, Bobby. When you have teenaged boys, husky boys, and doughnuts all in the same place, you're just asking for trouble.

> Hank Hill, *King of the Hill*

Listening

Kids, just because I don't care doesn't mean I'm not listening.

> Bart Simpson, *The Simpsons*

Literacy

DAVE BARRY: What are you reading?
TOMMY BARRY: A book.
DAVE: Good choice.

> *Dave's World*

Kelly, you gotta stay in school. It's important for your future. Now look at me. If I didn't have a high school diploma, I'd be— Well, maybe I'm not a good example. But it does help other people. Doctors, lawyers, astronauts. Everyone but me.

Al Bundy, *Married . . . with Children*

When I was a teenager I wanted to write the Great American Novel, but then I realized I didn't even want to read the Great American Novel.

Ray Barone, *Everybody Loves Raymond*

Living Life to the Fullest

I wanna shake off the dust of this one-horse town. I wanna explore the world. I wanna watch TV in a different time zone. I wanna visit strange, exotic malls. I'm sick of eating hoagies. I want a grinder, a sub, a foot-long hero. I want to LIVE, Marge. Won't you let me live? Won't you please?

Homer Simpson, *The Simpsons*

Love

You meet that special person. And you got a special love all saved up for them. That's the marrying kind of love. And that's the very best kind 'cause it comes from way down deep in your heart.

Andy Taylor, *The Andy Griffith Show*

Love is the only thing in life you've got to earn. Everything else you can steal.

> Pappy Maverick, *Maverick*

Please remember, and don't ever forget: It is better not to have been in love than never to have loved at all.

> Dwayne F. Schneider, *One Day at a Time*

Luck

If it wasn't for bad luck, I'd have no luck at all.

> George Jetson, *The Jetsons*

Magic

STEVEN KEATON: This is way too easy. What I really need is a straitjacket.
ELYSE KEATON: My sentiments exactly.

> *Family Ties*

For my grand finale magic act, I will proceed to make my wife disappear—a trick which any husband should appreciate.

> Herman Munster, *The Munsters*

Making a Fool of Yourself

DICK SOLOMON: Dr. Albright, have I been a perfect ass?
MARY ALBRIGHT: Aw, nobody's perfect.

> *3rd Rock from the Sun*

Making a Success of Yourself

Hey, honey, if you run into that assistant principal who said I'd never amount to anything—tell him Dr. Conner says hi.

> Dan Conner, *Roseanne*

Manliness

DICK SOLOMON: What about scratching?
HARRY SOLOMON: Outside the pants. Manly.
DICK: What about inside the pants?
HARRY: Too manly.

> *3rd Rock from the Sun*

Marriage

When somebody asks you to marry 'em, usually the polite thing to do is marry 'em right back.

> Andy Taylor, *The Andy Griffith Show*

Honey, please, we're already running an adoption agency, let's not start a matrimonial bureau.

> Alex Stone, *The Donna Reed Show*

GENE BERGMAN: So, I'm the one who's expendable?
ANNIE BERGMAN: Unfortunately, Gene, yes. Because I'm the only one who knows how to work the dishwasher!

> *Something Wilder*

RICKY RICARDO: Fred, I've got an awful problem on my hands.
FRED MERTZ: You should have thought about that before you married her.

> *I Love Lucy*

If you expect perpetual minute-to-minute romance from a marriage, you're in trouble.

> Steve Douglas, *My Three Sons*

A marriage is like a salad: The man has to know how to keep his tomatoes on the top.

> J.R. Ewing, *Dallas*

RICKY RICARDO: The whole thing is my fault. Something I said that started this whole mess.
LUCY RICARDO: What's that?
RICKY: I do.

> *I Love Lucy*

Okay, Robert, you want to know the advantages of marriage? Fine . . . You know when you fall asleep and you stop breathing? When you're married, there's always somebody there to nudge you back to life. . . . That's not a good example.

Ray Barone, *Everybody Loves Raymond*

I know this is painful for the ladies to hear, but if you get married, you have accepted the headship of a man, your husband. Christ is the head of the household and the husband is the head of the wife, and that's the way it is, period.

Pat Robertson, *700 Club*

It's not right for a man to be late to a wedding—especially his own.

Mike Brady, *The Brady Bunch*

Well how lucky can a man get? A wife who makes women sob and men dance through the streets.

Alex Stone, *The Donna Reed Show*

ERICA KANE: Adam, really. I know that you've been bored, but taking in Myrna Smythe? I mean, couldn't you have just taken in a dog from the pound?
ADAM CHANDLER: I prefer pure-bred bitches.
ERICA: Well, then you got what you wanted.

All My Children

MAGGIE SEAVER: You told me that total honesty is essential to a happy marriage.

JASON SEAVER: I said that after we were married.

   Growing Pains

It's a known fact that a little stone can derail a train. Us old married characters have to keep a constant watch for little stones on the track.

   Jim Anderson, *Father Knows Best*

Why can't somebody invent something for us to marry besides women?

   Fred Flintstone, *The Flintstones*

LUCY RICARDO: Mmmm. We have had fun, haven't we, honey?

RICKY RICARDO: Yessir. These fifteen years have been the best years of my life . . . What's the matter?

LUCY: We've only been married thirteen years.

RICKY: . . . What I mean is, it doesn't seem possible that all that fun could have been crammed into only thirteen years.

LUCY: Well, you certainly wormed your way out of that one.

   I Love Lucy

MR. SHEFFIELD: He can't make you happy.

FRAN: I don't wanna be happy. I wanna be married!

   The Nanny

Everybody, I have an announcement. Your happiness . . . sickens me. Everybody but me is looking at good times. But for me it's been one long continuous year since I got married. Actually, one long month. Helluary.

Al Bundy, *Married . . . with Children*

Matchmaking

MAN: So I said to my daughter, he's a fine boy. Steady job, gets meat wholesale, so she—

JIM ANDERSON: I know, she accused you of putting her on the auction block and selling her soul.

MAN: No. She jumped at the chance. Married him and he lost his job. I've been supporting him ever since. When will us fathers learn to keep our nose out of those things?

JIM: Probably never, Dave. At least, not as long as we're fathers.

Father Knows Best

Maternal Influence

You women must have a strong lobby. Even the songs about mothers are all gentle lullabies. The ones about dear old dad can be sung in bar rooms.

Alex Stone, *The Donna Reed Show*

Mechanical Ability

You can judge a boy's mechanical ability by the amount of grease you can get on him.

Ward Cleaver, *Leave It to Beaver*

Men vs. Women

Rob, everybody makes a fool of himself over a woman sooner or later, and I think the sooner the better.

Steve Douglas, *My Three Sons*

Always remember, and please never forget: A man is like a bow and arrow, and a woman is like a target. Bow and arrow needs practice. Target doesn't.

Dwayne F. Schneider, *One Day at a Time*

THEO HUXTABLE: Dad, it's not fair!
CLIFF HUXTABLE: What do you mean, it's not fair? There's two men living in a house with four women. We're lucky we have a gas station around the corner!

The Cosby Show

When a woman says nothing's wrong, *everything's wrong*. When a woman says *everything's wrong, everything's wrong*. And when a woman says *everything's wrong*, you'd better not laugh your ass off!

Homer Simpson, *The Simpsons*

Menstruation

DAN CONNER: Well, that's no reason for you to go running out of the room screaming like a maniac!
D.J. CONNER: It was about her having her period!
DAN: As you were.

Roseanne

HANK HILL: Bobby, every woman has a period . . . uh, of time . . . Every month . . .
BOBBY HILL: Even Mom?
HANK: (*sighs*) Bobby, if we're gonna get through this, you cannot ask me questions like that.

King of the Hill

Mistakes

A man's never wrong doing what he thinks is right!

Ben Cartwright, *Bonanza*

A fellow just hates to admit he's wrong. It takes a little courage to do it, and swallowing of pride, but it's one of the paths to wisdom.

      Jim Anderson, *Father Knows Best*

When you make a mistake, admit it. If you don't, you only make matters worse.

      Ward Cleaver, *Leave It to Beaver*

It takes a pretty big man to admit he's wrong.

      Jim Anderson, *Father Knows Best*

(*To his son*) A wrong decision is better than indecision. Now, get outta here before I shove that quotation book up your fat . . . !

      Tony Soprano, *The Sopranos*

Misunderstanding

MIKE STIVIC: You know, you are totally incomprehensible.
ARCHIE BUNKER: Maybe so, but I make a lot of sense.

      Archie Bunker, *All in the Family*

Money

Money speaks all languages.

      J.R. Ewing, *Dallas*

You don't ask for money back once you lend it out.

Dan Conner, *Roseanne*

Mothers-in-Law

Hey, Roseanne, I just saw all the animals in the neighborhood running in circles, so I guess that means your mother will be arriving soon.

Dan Conner, *Roseanne*

Music

But all the music you listen to is full of cussing. Why don't you listen to Marvin Gaye? He never swore—well, until his father shot him.

Michael Kyle, *My Wife and Kids*

Names

What's in a name anyway? In my day, no one went around calling themselves Chicanos or Mexican Americans or African Americans. We was all Americans. After that, if a guy was a Jig or a Spic, it was his own business.

Archie Bunker, *All in the Family*

When you name your daughter Rita, you should probably expect a slut.

    Harry Weston, *Empty Nest*

MIKE STIVIC: First of all, he's Polish, and second of all, how do you know the guy's not Russian or Jewish?
ARCHIE BUNKER: Ah, no. He ain't Jewish.
MIKE: Well, how do you know?
ARCHIE: Because his name is John. The Hebes don't name their kids John.

    All in the Family

LUCY RICARDO: I want the names to be unique and euphonious.
RICKY RICARDO: Okay. Unique if it's a boy and Euphonious if it's a girl.

    I Love Lucy

Narcissism

FLORIDA EVANS: You are a great father.
JAMES EVANS: Well, why you say it so surprised, baby? You knew the night you married me you had a great husband.

    Good Times

Neighbors

Some people say good fences make good neighbors. Some people say that good neighbors are good friends. Some people say love thy neighbor.

Tom Corbett, *The Courtship of Eddie's Father*

Well, you'll never find a more thoughtful neighbor. He even had the decency to croak during the day so that when the ambulance came, I was at work. Now that's class, brother!

Victor Pellet, *The In-Laws*

New York City

BARNEY MILLER: I'm sure getting robbed at knifepoint and spending half the night up here wasn't exactly what you had in mind when you decided to visit New York.

LADY: Well, it was better than seeing *Annie*.

Barney Miller

New York is a great place to visit, but when the visit is complicated by day-and-night legal conferences, it's a great place to leave for California and home.

Bentley Gregg, *Bachelor Father*

Nobility

While I'm unreasonable, do you have to be noble?

> Alex Stone, *The Donna Reed Show*

Obedience

RAY BARONE: All right, Ally, you have to do what Mommy says.
ALLY BARONE: Why?
RAY BARONE: 'Cause I do.

> *Everybody Loves Raymond*

Overeating

MARION CUNNINGHAM: Richie just hasn't got the appetite that Chuck has.
HOWARD CUNNINGHAM: Marion, Argentina hasn't got the appetite Chuck has.

> *Happy Days*

Pain

All of us hope to ease the pain of a loved one even though that's almost impossible.

> Grandpa "Zeb" Walton, *The Waltons*

Parents and Parenthood

When it comes to the fine art of parenting, mothers can do most things and fathers can do some things.

Jim, *Life According to Jim*

You know, what's funny about parenting is that you think what you're doing is the best thing and you really know inside that you have no clue what it is. I mean, even a dishwasher has a manual.

Tim Taylor, *Home Improvement*

CLAIRE HUXTABLE: (*exasperated*) Why do we have five children?
CLIFF HUXTABLE: Because we did not want to have six.

The Cosby Show

It's not easy to juggle a pregnant wife and a troubled child, but somehow I managed to fit in eight hours of TV a day.

Homer Simpson, *The Simpsons*

I don't care what kind of trouble you may get into in life—you don't ever need to be afraid to come to your parents and tell them.

Ward Cleaver, *Leave It to Beaver*

There comes a time when parents have to do what's right for them because they've earned it.

Jason Seaver, *Growing Pains*

This is Dr. Huxtable. I delivered some of you. I'm a parent and a taxpayer. And I am probably the only adult who will sue little children.

Cliff Huxtable, *The Cosby Show*

CATE HENNESSY: Are you okay?
PAUL HENNESSY: I'm mad at something you said.
CATE: What?
PAUL: Let's start a family.

8 Simple Rules . . . for Dating My Teenage Daughter

Parents are like cars . . . built-in obsolescence.

Harvey Lacey, *Cagney and Lacey*

Perfection

You can't expect to be perfect right off.

Jim Anderson, *Father Knows Best*

Perry Mason

I used to watch Perry Mason on TV all the time before he wound up in a wheelchair.

Archie Bunker, *Archie Bunker's Place*

Personal Conduct

People don't judge you by how you look but how you act.

Ward Cleaver, *Leave It to Beaver*

Personal Growth

Doesn't it feel good when you're just about to do something you know is wrong and you decide to do something else? Something that won't hurt you or anybody else? Doesn't that feel great? You know you're really growing then.

Fred Rogers, *Mister Rogers' Neighborhood*

Pets

You're glad to see me every minute of my life. I come home, you jump around and wag your tail. I go in the closet, I come out, you jump around and wag your tail. I turn my face away, I turn it back, you wag your tail. Either you love me very much or your short-term memory is shot.

Dr. Harry Weston, *Empty Nest*

A poodle? Why don't you just get me a cat and a sex-change operation?

Hank Hill, *King of the Hill*

Philosophy

Where would we be without the agitators of the world attaching the electrodes of knowledge to the nipples of ignorance?

Dick Solomon, *3rd Rock from the Sun*

It's like getting into a hot bath. You know: at first, you don't think you can take it. But then, you know, once you get all your luggage in, it's not that bad.

Ray Barone, *Everybody Loves Raymond*

Phone Interruptions

JIM ANDERSON: I never saw it to fail. Every time we sit down to eat the phone rings.
KATHY ANDERSON: I know how to stop it, Daddy.

JIM: How, Kitten?
KATHY: When the phone bill comes, don't pay it.
JIM: Not a bad idea.

Father Knows Best

Vanessa's Residence! No, she cannot come to the phone right now. Because it is now ten-oh-five, and she cannot take any calls past ten o'clock. No, I cannot take a message. I am her father. I am a doctor. I graduated from medical school, all right? Thank you for calling, this is a live voice.

Cliff Huxtable, *The Cosby Show*

Poetic Sayings

Not in the car,
not in the bar,
not in the house,
not up your blouse.
I cannot touch you here,
I cannot touch you there.
I cannot touch you
anywhere.

Dick Solomon, *3rd Rock from the Sun*

You caused the crash, now you've got to sling the hash.

Carl Winslow, *Family Matters*

Life is real, life is earnest.
If you're cold, turn up the furnace.

Herman Munster, *The Munsters*

I've seen her from the front, I've seen her from the back.
I've seen her in a chair, I've seen her in a sack.
I've seen her stand. I've seen her crouch.
I've seen her on her stupid couch.
I do not like her in the mall,
I do not like her in the hall.
I do not like her in my life.
I do not like my big red wife.

Al Bundy, *Married . . . with Children*

I can't deny,
I think I might cry,
because I still don't know,
who ate my pie!

Michael Kyle, *My Wife and Kids*

Politics

Cliff Barnes just broke the cardinal rule of politics—never get caught in bed with a live man or a dead woman.

J.R. Ewing, *Dallas*

These candidates make me want to vomit in terror.

Homer Simpson, *The Simpsons*

Power

Power isn't something you earn. Real power is something you take.

Jock Ewing, *Dallas*

Practical Advice

Another thing children learn as they grow is how to urinate and make bowel movements—BMs—in the toilet instead of their diapers. Urine and BMs come out of our bodies. They're things our bodies don't need.

Fred Rogers, *Mr. Rogers' Neighborhood*

If you can't fight 'em, and they won't let you join 'em, best get out of the country.

Pappy Maverick, *Maverick*

Prayer in School

You see what happened in 1962? They took prayer out of the schools. The next year the Supreme Court ordered Bible reading taken from the schools. And then, progressing, liberals, most of them athcistic educators, have pushed to remove all religion from the lives of children. The people who wrote the "Humanist Manifesto" and their pupils and their disciples are in charge of education in America today.

Pat Robertson, *700 Club*

Pregnancy

DAN CONNER: You should have known it was your fertile time.
ROSEANNE CONNER: Well, excuse me for ovulating.

Roseanne

Prejudice

ARCHIE BUNKER: Oh no . . . oh no, I'm gonna sue that guy. First thing in the morning, I'm gonna get myself a good Jew lawyer.

MIKE STIVIC: Archie, do you always have to label people? Why can't you just get a lawyer? Why does it have to be a Jewish lawyer?

ARCHIE: 'Cause when I'm gonna sue an Arab, I'm gonna get a guy that's full of hate.

All in the Family

What the hell kind of country is this if I can only hate a man if he's white?

Hank Hill, *King of the Hill*

MIKE STIVIC: Just because a guy is sensitive and wears glasses, you make him out to be a queer.

ARCHIE BUNKER: I never said a guy who wears glasses is a queer. A guy who wears glasses is a four-eyes. A guy who's a fag is a queer.

All in the Family

Premenstrual Syndrome

It's like a twenty-four-hour roller-coaster ride with Sybil at the switch.

Dan Conner, *Roseanne*

But you can't actually say that to 'em or else they'll kill you. And they're allowed to, see, it's that whole period, PMS thing. I don't know—I'm not a doctor—but I think that PMS stands for "Pummels Men's Scrotums."

Al Bundy, *Married . . . with Children*

Pride

I'm not proud of everything I've done. I'm not proud of having a poor education. I'm not proud of being dyslexic. I'm not proud of being an alcoholic drug addict. I'm not proud of biting the head off a bat. I'm not proud of having attention deficit disorder. But I'm a real guy. To be Ozzy Osbourne, it could be worse. I could be Sting.

Ozzy Osbourne, *The Osbournes*

Privacy

Always respect the privacy of others.

Tom Corbett, *The Courtship of Eddie's Father*

FRED SANFORD: If you wanna be down here with that girl, that's your business. I mean, if you wanna be hugging and kissing all night, that's your business.
LAMONT SANFORD: I appreciate it—

FRED: But when she smacks your face and the police come in here and arrest me for harboring a sex maniac, then that's MY business. So you get her the hell out of here.

Sanford and Son

Promises

LOIS GRIFFIN: Peter, what did you promise me?
PETER GRIFFIN: That I wouldn't drink at the party.
LOIS: And what did you do?
PETER: Drank at the pa— Whoa! I almost walked into that one.

Family Guy

Public Education

PHILLIP DRUMMOND: Why public school? You sure know how to surprise a father. You know what public school can be like. Crime. Drugs. Kids getting ripped off.
KIMBERLY DRUMMOND: Willis and Arnold go to public school.
PHILLIP: Well, that's different. They're boys.
KIMBERLY: You see that: You're discriminating against me.
ARNOLD JACKSON: Yeah, why can't she have the same disadvantages we have?

Diff'rent Strokes

Punishment

What she done was wrong, and she gotta be punished. For the next two weeks, no out after school. No out at all. If you find yourself having fun at something, stop it. And no delicious foods for three weeks. You only gotta eat the terrible foods that are good for you. And then no TV for a week. And the next week—and this is gonna be tougher—educational TV only.

Archie Bunker, *All in the Family*

Quitting

Over? What are you talking about? What kind of talk is that? It's un-American! Did George W. Bush quit even after losing the popular vote? No. Did he quit after losing millions of dollars of his father's money in failed oil companies? No! Did he quit after knocking that girl up? No! Did he quit after he got that DUI? No. Did he quit after he got busted for drunk and disorderly conduct at a football game? No. Did he quit . . .

Peter Griffin, *Family Guy*

Ronald Reagan

ANDREW KEATON: Alex is reading me *Robin Hood*, where he robs from the poor and gives to the rich.

STEVEN KEATON: That's not Robin Hood, that's Ronald Reagan.
Family Ties

Refined Women

FELIX UNGER: I like my women quiet, ladylike, attractive and refined.
OSCAR MADISON: What for?
The Odd Couple

Religion

When the missionaries went into darkest Africa to bring God to the natives, do you think they asked their permission? Like hell. They dragged 'em out of the trees and right down to the river and they held them under there until they seen the light. And the natives was glad about that 'cause that's how they found God, and then later when they was chained to the bottom of the slave ship they were happy 'cause they had someone to pray to, which proves that for everyone's own good you gotta use force. That's the Christian way.

Archie Bunker, *All in the Family*

D.J. CONNER: What religion are we?
ROSEANNE CONNER: I have no idea. Dan?

DAN CONNER: Well . . . My mom's mom was Pentecostal and Baptist on the side of my dad. Your mom's mom was Lutheran, and her dad was Jewish.

D.J.: So what do we believe?

ROSEANNE: Well . . . We believe in . . . being good. So basically, we're good people.

DAN: Yeah, but we're not practicing.

Roseanne

Convictions and beliefs. What do they have to do with religion?

Tim Taylor, *Home Improvement*

Respect

When a man carries a gun all the time, the respect he thinks he's getting might actually be fear. So I don't carry a gun because I don't want the people of Mayberry to fear a gun. I'd rather they respect me.

Andy Taylor, *The Andy Griffith Show*

Respect is for the dead. The living need dough.

Archie Bunker, *All in the Family*

You think I didn't respect you, Christine, but the truth is, I didn't even think of you.

Coach Hayden Fox, *Coach*

HOMER SIMPSON: Son, about last night. You might've noticed Daddy acting a little strange, and you probably don't understand why.

BART SIMPSON: I understand why: You were wasted.

HOMER: I'm sorry it happened, and I just hope you didn't lose a lot of respect for me.

BART: Dad, I have as much respect for you as I ever did or ever will.

HOMER: Aww.

The Simpsons

Revenge

Now you go to Supreme Salvage and pick up some bathtubs I ordered. Here's a check. Now listen, if you try to run off with my truck and try to cash my check, I'll find you. It may take a week, it may take a month, it might take me years, but one day—maybe fifty years from now—you'll be walkin' down the street, and when you least expect it, a hundred-fifteen-year-old man gonna jump out of the alley with a two-by-four and cave your skull in.

Fred Sanford, *Sanford and Son*

The world is littered with the bodies of people who have tried to stick it to ol' J.R. Ewing.

J.R. Ewing, *Dallas*

What's the matter with revenge? It's the perfect way to get even!

      Archie Bunker, *All in the Family*

Richard Nixon

Let me tell you one thing about Richard E. Nixon. He knows how to keep his wife, Pat, home. Roosevelt could never do that with Eleanor. She was always out on the loose. Runnin' around with the coloreds. Tellin' them they was getting the short end of the stick. She was the one that discovered the coloreds in this country, we never knew they was there.

      Archie Bunker, *All in the Family*

Romance

That's your idea of a romantic dinner, Oscar? Red wine and fish?

      Felix Unger, *The Odd Couple*

Rules

I don't follow rules, especially my own.

      Luke Spencer, *General Hospital*

If you can quote the rules, then you can obey them.

Tony Soprano, *The Sopranos*

Salesmen

Even salesmen know instinctively it's the woman who has to be pleased.

Alex Stone, *The Donna Reed Show*

Salt

HAZEL BURKE: Is this salty enough?
GEORGE BAXTER: (*exasperated*) I don't care anything about salt.
DOROTHY BAXTER: You do too. You're very finicky about salt.

Hazel

School

PRINCIPAL: I'm sure your children will be very happy here.
GOMEZ ADDAMS: If we'd wanted them to be happy, we would've let them stay at home.

The Addams Family

Sometimes I just wish I were Ozzie Nelson. He'd just say "Go to college"—and that would be the end of that.

Howard Cunningham, *Happy Days*

Second Jobs

Peg, let me state this as clearly as I can: I would rather rip off my nose with a can opener. I would rather bob for apples in a sewer. I would rather have a catheter the size of a garden hose before I get another job to pay for your shopping.

Al Bundy, *Married . . . with Children*

Secrets

There comes a time when a secret isn't a secret anymore.

Grandpa "Zeb" Walton, *The Waltons*

Self-Improvement

MEL SHARPELS: I like myself the way I am. Who needs self-improvement?

ALICE HYATT: Anyone who likes you the way you are.

Alice

Senility

But every time I learn something new, it pushes out something old. Remember that time I took a home wine-making course and forgot how to drive?

Homer Simpson, *The Simpsons*

Separation of Church and State

That was never in the Constitution, however much the liberals laugh at me for saying it, they know good and well it was never in the Constitution! Such language only appeared in the constitution of the Communist Soviet Union.

Pat Robertson, *700 Club*

Sex

MARY ALBRIGHT: When men get gray hair they look distinguished. When women get gray hair they look old.

DICK SOLOMON: When women get breasts they look sexy. When men get breasts they look old.

MARY: Good point.

3rd Rock from the Sun

Nothing brings out the woman in the woman more than the man in the man.

> Gomez Addams, *The Addams Family*

PHILLIP BANKS: No sex before marriage, Will.
WILL SMITH: Come on, Uncle Phil. This is the nineties.
PHILLIP: Try a cold shower.
WILL: I've been doing that since the eighties. It don't work no more.

> *The Fresh Prince of Bel-Air*

All part of my master plan to avoid having sex with my wife. See, first I take her to Denny's. She stuffs herself so full of popcorn shrimp, she lists to one side.

> Al Bundy, *Married . . . with Children*

JIM ANDERSON: What'll we do?
MARGARET ANDERSON: All we can do is to get his mind off it.

> *Father Knows Best*

GLORIA STIVIC: Admit it, Daddy, your whole generation is afraid of sex.
ARCHIE BUNKER: Ah, listen, little girl, if I was afraid of it, you wouldn't be here. Right, Edith? (*pause*) Right, Edith?
EDITH BUNKER: I'm trying to remember.

> *All in the Family*

Son, let this be a lesson to you: Never do tequilla shooters within a country mile of a marriage chapel.

  Al Bundy, *Married . . . with Children*

ARCHIE BUNKER: When your mother-in-law and me was goin' around together, it was two years. . . . We never . . . I never . . . I mean, absolutely nothin', not until the wedding night.
EDITH BUNKER: Yeah, and even then.

  All in the Family

Those articles that say married couples have sex every month are just sensationalistic lies perpetrated on the public to sell magazines. It's hooey, I tell you, hooey.

  Al Bundy, *Married . . . with Children*

LOUISE JEFFERSON: George, I'm flattered. After all these years, you still can't wait.
GEORGE JEFFERSON: It's not that. It's just that if I wait too long, I'll miss Johnny Carson.
LOUISE: Johnny Carson, huh? Then I'll have two men in the bedroom to make me laugh.

  The Jeffersons

(*To wife, Sue Ellen*) Well, I'll be damned if you can come in here anytime you want and use me like some stud service!

  J.R. Ewing, *Dallas*

If you want to have sex, the kids have to leave, and if you want it to be good, *you* have to leave.

Al Bundy, *Married . . . with Children*

Sex Education

[Planned Parenthood] is teaching kids to fornicate, teaching people to have adultery, every kind of bestiality, homosexuality, lesbianism—everything that the Bible condemns.

Pat Robertson, *700 Club*

Shaving

CLIFF HUXTABLE: Just promise me you won't lose the razor in there.

THEO HUXTABLE: I put on too much, didn't I?

CLIFF: Oh, no. Sometimes I use three or four cans myself.

The Cosby Show

Shopping

D.J. CONNER: Do we have to go to the Big and Fat store?

DAN CONNER: It's big and *tall*, D.J.

Roseanne

Shows of Affection

Bobby, if you weren't my son, I'd hug you.
>Hank Hill, *King of the Hill*

Sibling Rivalry

Brothers and sisters fighting is as natural as a white man's dialogue in a Spike Lee movie.
>Peter Griffin, *Family Guy*

Smoking

LAMONT SANFORD: Pop, since you was ten you smoked a cigarette forty-one miles long.
FRED SANFORD: That's real super king-sized, ain't it?
LAMONT: Forty-one miles. That's like you smoked a cigarette from here to Disneyland.
>*Sanford and Son*

Social Status

Boy, folks sure are getting uppity. Eating roast beef for supper and it ain't even the weekend.
>Andy Taylor, *The Andy Griffith Show*

Sorrow

ROB PETRIE: Oh, honey, please, I hate to see you cry like this.
LAURA PETRIE: Well, that's the only way I know how to cry.

The Dick Van Dyke Show

Spankings

[Elroy has broken one of Jane's favorite vases. George is congratulating her on not getting mad immediately.]

GEORGE JETSON: And because you kept cool, you warmed his heart.
JANE JETSON: I'd prefer to warm his bottom.

The Jetsons

JED CLAMPETT: Boy, I'm gonna give you twenty-four hours to clean up all this mess.
JETHRO BODINE: Aw come on, Uncle Jed. I'm gonna clean up. I'm gonna set this world on fire!
JED: You're gonna clean up alright. Everything. Or you're gonna end up with the seat of your britches on fire.

The Beverly Hillbillies

Sports

Son, when you participate in sporting events, it's not whether you win or lose, it's how drunk you get.

Homer Simpson, *The Simpsons*

Starting the Day Off Right

What a beautiful day—the kind of day that starts with a hearty breakfast and ends with a newsreader saying " . . . before turning the gun on himself."

Dan Conner, *Roseanne*

Stealing

It ain't stealing—not when you take it from work.

Archie Bunker, *All in the Family*

Stereotypes

ARCHIE BUNKER: If God had intended whites and coloreds to dance together—
MIKE STIVIC: He'd have given us rhythm too.

All in the Family

Stolen Vehicles

Hello, police? I'd like to describe a . missing person. How tall? About four feet tall, five feet wide. Smoke belching out the rear, weighs two tons. No, it's not Oprah. No, it's not Delta Burke. Who'd call to report her missing? No, it's my Dodge.

Al Bundy, *Married . . . with Children*

Stupidity

The only way you could ever have a high IQ is to go up in a blimp.

Uncle Martin, *My Favorite Martian*

If brains was lard, Jethro couldn't grease a pan.

The Beverly Hillbillies

Give it enough time and everyone says something stupid.

George Jefferson, *The Jeffersons*

I may be an idiot, but at least I don't hide it from you.

Carl Winslow, *Family Matters*

Success

KATHY WILLIAMS: Show me a successful man and I'll show you a woman behind him.
DANNY WILLIAMS: That's just where she belongs.
   Make Room for Daddy (The Danny Thomas Show)

Surgeons

All them surgeons—they're highway robbers. Why do you think they wear masks when they work on you?
   Archie Bunker, *All in the Family*

Sympathy

Oh, poor baby. What do you want, a Whitman's Sampler?
   Tony Soprano, *The Sopranos*

Table Manners

FELIX UNGER: Do you always talk with your mouth full?
OSCAR MADISON: Only when I'm eating.
   The Odd Couple

Taxes

A penny earned is a penny taxed
    Andy Taylor, *The Andy Griffith Show*

Teasing

Son, you're teasin' the gorilla in the monkey house.
    Hank Hill, *King of the Hill*

Teenagers

No fourteen-year-old boy should have a ninety-five-dollar shirt unless he's on stage with his four brothers.
    Cliff Huxtable, *The Cosby Show*

When you're a teenager you automatically expect the world to cave in on you at any moment.
    Ward Cleaver, *Leave It to Beaver*

Trading In a Car

It would be like losing one of you or, Peg, it would be like trading you in for a young blonde with new, smooth, factory-warrantied hooters. Sure, the first few rides would be nice, but in the long run—and this, Peg, is what depresses me every day—I realize that . . . you're the one I want.

Al Bundy, *Married . . . with Children*

The Unavoidable

I guess there's two things that'll always be in the world—dirt and homework.

Ward Cleaver, *Leave It to Beaver*

Unpleasantness

It may not be bitter wine, but there sure is a bad taste to it.

Blake Carrington, *Dynasty*

Vacation

WARD CLEAVER: Ah, two whole weeks with nothing to do but lay around fishing . . . sunning . . . What a life!

JUNE CLEAVER: While I'm cooking the meals, doing the dishes, making the bed, cleaning the cabin.

WARD: Yeah, what a life!

Leave It to Beaver

Valentine's Day

PAUL BUCHMAN: Why is it I love you any more in the middle of February than on, say, August 21st? You know, to me, every day with you is Valentine's Day.
JAMIE BUCHMAN: So, in other words, you forgot to buy me a card.
PAUL: That's what I'm saying.

Mad About You

Waiters

When the waiter knows your name, that's absolute proof that you're a man of the world.

Ward Cleaver, *Leave It to Beaver*

Wanting What You Can't Have

RICKY RICARDO: There you go again, wanting something that you haven't got.
LUCY RICARDO: I do not. I just want to see what I haven't got that I don't want.

I Love Lucy

Wealth

Your mother and I are rich. You have nothing.

    Cliff Huxtable, *The Cosby Show*

Welfare

LAMONT SANFORD: Pop, that's what the welfare thing was set up for . . . poor people. The have-nots.

FRED SANFORD: The have-nots? Well, if the have-nots could get something from the haves and the haves gave the have-nots half of what they have, then the haves would still be the haves and the have-nots would be the have-somethings.

    Sanford and Son

Winning

All that matters is winning.

    J.R. Ewing, *Dallas*

Winning a Woman's Heart

CLIFF HUXTABLE: We always get our women.

CLAIRE HUXTABLE: Yes, but not because of the things you do; despite them.

    The Cosby Show

ALEX STONE: I know you're sensitive to the word, but how else do you describe a woman who stays home, runs a house, cooks, cleans and looks after the kids.

DONNA STONE: How about *mule*?

> *The Donna Reed Show*

(*To his wife*) You should be a very happy woman. You're beautiful, you got a nice home, three great kids, a husband who adores you. That oughta be enough for any gal.

> Danny Williams, *Make Room for Daddy*
> (*The Danny Thomas Show*)

Woman's Work

Washing dishes, making beds, and cooking hardly qualifies a person to be a building contractor.

> Jim Anderson, *Father Knows Best*

HARRIET NELSON: You know, if they let women in the fire department, then I'd see more of you.

OZZIE: Are you kidding? You gals take too long to dress.

> *The Adventures of Ozzie and Harriet*

Women

A good toaster is like a good woman. Treat her right and she'll keep you warm and happy in your old age.

    Fred Horton, *Lou Grant*

A stirred up bunch of women can save almost anything except money.

    Mike Brady, *The Brady Bunch*

DICK SOLOMON: Women. You can't live with 'em and you can't have heterosexual sex without 'em.

HARRY SOLOMON: Women. You can't live with 'em and yet they're everywhere.

    3rd Rock from the Sun

DAN CONNER: (*to brother-in-law Fred*) Damn women! Who do they think they are anyway?

ROSEANNE CONNER: We're sugar and spice and everything nice. So bite me!

    Roseanne

Work

GRANDPA "ZEB" WALTON: I don't believe a person should have more than they know what to do with. I believe a body should earn his living by the sweat of his brow.

JOHN WALTON: I don't know, Pa. There are times I could use a little less sweat on my brow.

The Waltons

My old pappy used to say, "Son, hard work never hurt anyone—who didn't do it."

Bart Maverick, *Maverick*

BURT CAMPBELL: I'm building a future so you can have everything you ever wanted. . . . I need to do it for me, to prove I can do it.

MARY CAMPBELL: Tomorrow when you're driving home and some drunk jumps over the center of the divider and you wind up dead, you will have spent the last days and nights of your life working.

Soap

Early to bed and early to rise is the curse of the working class.

Pappy Maverick, *Maverick*

Don't impose too long on a man's hospitality: he's liable to put you to work.

> Pappy Maverick, *Maverick*

DICK SOLOMON: Nina, take my car into the garage and rotate my tires.
SECRETARY: That's not in my job description.
DICK: What's in your job description?
SECRETARY: Typing.
DICK: Okay, well type it in your job description, and get my tires rotated.

> *3rd Rock from the Sun*

WARD CLEAVER: (*arriving home from the office*) Hi.
JUNE CLEAVER: Hi. You didn't bring your briefcase home.
WARD: Well, of course not. I was the last one to leave the office.
JUNE: What does that have to do with it?
WARD: What's the use of lugging a briefcase home if there's no one there to see how conscientious you are.
JUNE: What are you going to do Monday morning?
WARD: I guess I'll just have to be the first one at the office.

> *Leave It to Beaver*

THELMA EVANS: Okay, speedy, so how much are you getting paid?
J.J. EVANS: The man said this is a wonderful opportunity. Salary is not important.

JAMES EVANS: That's what they've been telling me all my life, and they prove it by what they pay me.

Good Times

The World

The problem in the world today is communication. Too much communication.

Homer Simpson, *The Simpsons*

Youth Fashion

PAUL HENNESSY: Hold it. I can see your bra and that slingshot you're wearing.

KERRY HENNESSY: Must be casual-sex day at school.

BRIDGETT HENNESSY: It's a thong.

PAUL: It's floss.

8 Simple Rules . . . for Dating My Teenage Daughter

Pull that skirt down. Every time you sit down in one of them things, the mystery's over.

Archie Bunker, *All in the Family*

Acknowledgments

Like the matinee idol with his name emblazoned across a cinema marquee, it is the writer who gets the credit on the cover of a book, even though the process is a collaborative one. In my case, there were many collaborators, and I would like to express my deepest thanks and gratitude to each of them now.

My unbelievable editor and pop culture kindred spirit at Kensington Publishing, Gary Goldstein, whose wisdom, guidance, and friendship offered bedrock support through the six months it took to research and write this book. From taking a chance on a first-time author to helping midwife the finished manuscript with minimal labor pains, Gary has proven to be a dream come true in every sense of the word—not to mention, a man who knows more about classic TV than even I ever thought possible.

My devoted literary agent, advisor, and friend, Peter Rubie, for believing in me and never losing faith, despite the five years that it took to get a return on his investment.

My incredible family—Holly and Gabe Coltea; Porter and Carol Rodgers; Brent, Melissa, Emilie, Elizabeth, Caroline, and Abigail Padgett; Melinda, John, Jack, Hank, and Frederick Couzens; Susan, Greg, Charlie, and John Drumm; Heyward and Sherrill Whetsell; Alva and Libby Whetsell; Bob and Elsie Stevens; and Lucia Schuler, as well as their children and grandchildren, for enduring—and, for some inexplicable reason, even encouraging—their oddball relative's lifelong obsession with television.

My late grandparents, Bill and Elizabeth Whetsell—Granddaddy for being one of the best friends I've ever had, and Grandmother for passing along her love of the written word.

To my late maternal grandmother, Fern Rodgers, my great aunt Helen, my Uncle Dan, Uncle Heyward and Aunt Elsie, Uncle Bub and Aunt Lois, for the cherished memories of each of you I will always carry in my heart.

My beloved friends old and new—especially the incredibly gorgeous and exceptionally talented diva extraordinaire, Ann Anello—and Ann, Michele Philippe, Rob and Laura Befumo, Jeffrey Gurian, Ernie Savage and Jennifer Fish, Martin and Joan Camins, Dick and Eleanor Brubaker, Wayne Jacques, Rob Bates, Mitch Kerper, Bruce and Carolyn Coplin, Marty Fischer, Mike Kornfeld, Gary and Rene Susman, Richard Rubenstein, Ted Farone, Maureen Langan, Ruth Zimmerman Klatzko, Cynthia Crane and Carol Scibelli—for their laughter and love.

My mentors, colleagues, and editors over the years—especially Marsha Della-Guistina at Emerson College; John Strahinich at the *Boston Herald*; Jack Thomas at *The Boston Globe*; author Ron Suskind; Bob Heisler, Graham Fuller, and David Bianculli at the New York *Daily News*; Gary Shapiro at *The New York Sun*; and Brad Hamilton, Mike Shane, Michael Starr, Debra Birnbaum and Faye Penn at the *New York Post*—for bylines, paychecks, encouragement, and teaching me the tricks of the trade.

The staff of the Museum of Television & Radio in New York, for help in research and answering endless questions.

My extended family at the New York Friars Club for giving me many hours of refuge, laughter, and fun.

My wonderfully supportive parents, Anne and Bill Whetsell, for their sacrifices and making me immensely proud to call them mom and dad.

And last—but certainly not least—special thanks to Sharon Klein (and her terrific parents, Murray and Ozzie, who brought her into this world), for joint custody of the greatest dog in the world, our treasured Maltese, Max, and for being an extraordinary human being who amazes and inspires me every day. I love you with all my heart.